Seedtime Stories
Bedtime Stories, Poems, & Devotionals

Beverly Capps Burgess

A
Little
Lamb
Book

Burgess Publishing, Inc.
Broken Arrow, Oklahoma

Seedtime Stories
ISBN 1-879470-01-2
Copyright © 1991 by
Beverly Capps Burgess
P.O. Box 520
Broken Arrow, OK 74013

Published by
Burgess Publishing, Inc.
P.O. Box 520
Broken Arrow, OK 74013
U.S.A.

Dedication

This book is for Zac and all of the friends he has influenced for Christ. Zac, may you always be in the center of God's will for your life.

Contents

Foreword

The stories in this book are designed to help you be like the seed planted in a good field. You can learn to watch out for problems that would make you discouraged or lead you away from God. If you know how to avoid them, then you can be strong in the Lord and your life will be happy as you learn to put God first.

Beverly Capps Burgess

Chapter One

The Parable of the Sower
(Mark 4: 1-20)

Jesus taught people by parables. Parables are stories that teach a lesson. One day Jesus was teaching the people by a lake. The crowd gathered around Him so closely that He decided to get into a boat and teach from the water. The people stood by the water's edge listening to the parable of the sower. Later on the disciples asked Jesus to explain the parable to them. This is what Jesus said:

"The Word of God is like seed that a farmer plants in the ground. Some people are like the seed that falls along the pathway. Satan comes to steal that seed with troubles and they don't last.

Other people hear God's Word and get

1

really excited. They think it sounds wonderful, but they are like plants that have no roots. When trouble comes their way, they decide the Word of God doesn't work. They don't last very long because they are like seed sown on rocky ground.

Others hear the Word and are like seed sown among the weeds. They begin to believe the Word of God and grow, but the weeds (cares of this world, deceitfulness of riches, desire for other things) grow also and choke the Word of God. Then it doesn't produce any fruit or success.

People who are like seed planted in a good field are the ones we should be like. They hear the Word of God, they study the Bible, and when Satan comes with troubles or cares they believe God's Word anyway. They are doers of the Word. Soon they have a beautiful crop, thirty, sixty, or even one hundred times the number of seeds that were planted."

In the stories that follow you will see how things can come between you and God. Jesus warned us about these things in the parable we just read. If you know how to avoid the cares of this world, deceitfulness of riches, and desire for other things, then you can serve God better. So pay close attention and find out what happened to Timothy, Kristen, Daniel and Jeffery!

Seed Sown Among Thorns

And the cares of this world,
and the deceitfulness of riches,
and the lusts of other things
entering in, choke the word,
and it becometh unfruitful.

Mark 4:19

Chapter Two
The Cares of This World

Timothy's Prayer

"Timothy," called Mother, "would you please come in the house?"

"Oh no," thought Timothy. "I wanted to ride my bike. I hope Mother doesn't make me stay in and clean my room."

When Timothy walked in and saw his mother's smiling face he knew she must have good news. "Timothy, Paul's mother called and asked if you could come and play with Paul for the afternoon. Would you like to go?"

"Sure, Mom! Can I ride my bike over to his house?"

"Yes, you may," said Mother, "if you remember to be very careful and look both ways when you cross the street."

"Thanks, Mom!" exclaimed Timothy and he ran outside to begin the short ride to Paul's house.

The closer Timothy came to Paul's house the more he wondered if Paul's dad would be home. He overheard the neighbors talking about what a mean man he was. He didn't even go to church anymore. "Maybe what those people said isn't even true. I can't imagine having a mean dad. Oh well, it's the middle of the day and I'm sure he won't be home anyway."

Timothy arrived at Paul's house. It wasn't as nice as his home but Timothy knew it was what was inside a person that counted, not how big or pretty his house was.

As Timothy knocked on the door he heard footsteps inside. Paul's mom opened the door. "Paul's in his room waiting for you," she said with a smile. "We were both so glad your mom said you could come over today. Paul doesn't have a lot of friends but he really enjoys playing with you."

"Hey, Timothy! come here," called Paul from the back of the house. "I want to show you my room. I have a new boat we can play with in the sink."

"Great!" said Timothy as he hurried toward the sound of Paul's voice.

6

Paul and Tim played together almost all afternoon. They even found some other children to join in a game of baseball. What fun they had! Paul hit a home run at the end of the game. Both boys ran in the house to tell Paul's mother that they had won. She was as excited as they were. "How about cookies and milk for you two?" she asked.

"Yes ma'am! That would be great," they replied.

Just as Timothy ate his last bite of the huge chocolate chip cookie he  heard a car door slam. Then he heard footsteps coming up the walk. The front door swung open. It slammed shut so hard that the glass rattled. In came Paul's dad. With a scowl on his face he said, "What are you doing eating cookies this time of day? Don't you know better than that, boy?"

"But Dad, we won the...."

"I don't care what you won, get out of here now. I'm hungry. Where is my supper?"

Paul held back the tears and said to Tim, "I think you should go home now. Maybe I can come to your house sometime. OK?"

"Sure," replied Timothy as he gently closed the door.

Timothy felt so sad inside as he rode home on his bike. He didn't know what to do but he knew he had to find some way to help Paul's dad.

When he arrived home, Mom asked, "Did you have fun today, Tim?"

Tim spoke slowly, "Yes ma'am, I guess so...."

"Why honey, what's wrong? Did Paul upset you?"

"No, Paul and I had a great time. But Paul's dad...well.... I don't know how to change it, but it's terrible."

"What are you talking about, Tim?"

"Well, Mom, Paul told me his dad isn't a Christian. He treats him and his mom really bad sometimes. His home isn't like ours. Our home is really peaceful and nice. You and Dad really love me and each other. I never knew I had it so good. I really like Paul a lot and I've just got to help him...but how?"

Mother sat down and said, "Paul, you are about to learn a very important lesson. This will help you the rest of your life if you will remember what I am about to tell you." Then she explained, "There are many times in our lives when we encounter things we want to change. Some of them we just change ourselves because they are easy, and others take more than that." As she reached for her Bible on the table she continued, "God gave us an important tool to use. Prayer is that tool. When you pray, things can change. Sometimes you will have to be diligent and stand firm for your change to come. But God says when we pray, He will answer us. Matthew 18:18-20 says, 'Verily I say unto you, Whatsoever ye bind on earth shall be bound in heaven: and whatsoever ye shall loose on earth shall be loosed in heaven. Again I say unto you, That if two of you shall agree on earth as touching anything that they shall ask, it shall be done for them of my Father which is in heaven. For where two or three are gathered together in my name, there I am in the midst of them.'"

As Mother closed her Bible, Timothy asked, "Mom, can we do that now? I mean the two of us pray and agree that Paul's dad would come to know Christ and have a change of heart."

"Yes, Tim," Mother answered, "we certainly can."

Timothy began to pray, "Dear God, I ask You to help Paul's dad to know You so Paul can have a happy home like mine. I believe what Your Word says and I know You want Paul's dad to be happy, too. Thank You for hearing and answering my prayer. Amen."

Days and weeks went by and still Paul's dad was the same. In fact, Timothy had heard some people say he was worse than ever. They even said he might lose his job because of his temper. Timothy was tempted to give up and forget his special prayer. But he remembered his mother saying, "Sometimes you will have to stand firm for your change to come." "I'm not giving up," he thought.

Just then the telephone rang and Timothy answered it.

"Hold on a minute, Paul, I'll ask my mom," he said.

"Mom," called Tim, "May I please spend the night at Paul's tonight; his mom says it is OK, please?"

"All right," Mom answered, "if you promise not to stay up too late."

"Thanks, Mom," Tim said as he picked up the phone.

"Paul, Mom said 'yes.' I'll be over in a few minutes. Bye."

As Timothy packed his suitcase he realized he would see Paul's dad if he spent the night. "What if he screams and yells again?" he thought. "I will be so scared! Maybe I should stay home." Finally, he decided to go and hope for the best. After all, he had prayed and maybe the man had changed.

When Tim arrived at Paul's they put up a tent in the backyard. They played all afternoon in the tent. It made a great hideout. The boys thought about how much fun it would be to

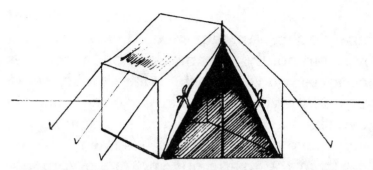

sleep in the backyard. Paul said to Tim, "Why don't you ask because you're company. Mom would probably say 'yes' to you."

"But it's your house and your mom, and I think you should ask," Tim argued.

Finally, they decided to go in and ask together. Paul spoke up, "Mom, uh...could we...I mean, do you think...well, we want to know if we can sleep in the backyard?"

Mother answered quickly, "You know you will have to talk to your dad about that. If I were you I would wait and see what kind of a mood he is in when he comes home. Dinner is ready so wash and come sit down."

Just then the door swung open and Paul's dad stormed in. "Nobody in this world cares!" he screamed. "I've worked for that company ten years and they fire me! They say I'm not doing my job. Now what am I supposed to do? They don't care if we starve to death. I tell you, there is no one in this world who cares what happens to me!"

There was silence in the room. Paul's dad began to sob. Tim remembered his prayer and spoke up boldly, "I know Someone who cares and loves you very much." He moved closer to him and continued, "God loves you so much He gave His only Son, Jesus, to die for you so you could have everlasting life. Jesus will change you from the inside out and make your life happy."

Paul's dad reached out to Tim and gave him a big hug. Then he put the boy on his lap and said, "Tim, tell me more about God and His Son, Jesus. I really do want to make Him Lord of my life."

Tim smiled a big smile at Paul and his mom. Somehow, sleeping in that tent wasn't very important, anymore.

The Cares of This World Devotional
Mark 16:15

Paul's dad let the cares of this world keep him from Christ. He didn't receive Christ until someone began to pray for him.

Timothy was very brave. He knew he had the answer that Paul's dad was looking for. He was not afraid of what anyone might say. He prayed and believed God for an answer. God did answer his prayer. God will answer your prayers also.

Sometimes people want to tell others about Jesus but they are afraid of what their friends might say. If we want to please God, we cannot worry about what our friends will say. We should always do what will please God. That is what is most important. God will teach you how to witness. In Mark chapter 16, verse 15 Jesus told us to preach the Gospel to every creature. Preaching the Gospel means to share Jesus with others and you are never too young to start!

Pray This Prayer Today....

Father,

Please help me to be brave in sharing Jesus with others. I believe Your Word and I will be obedient to You. Help me never to be afraid of what other people say about me. If my friends make fun of me I will pray for them. I won't be upset by them. Thank You for helping me to win others to Jesus. I love You...

In Jesus' Name. Amen

I Have Nothing To Worry About

You protect me day and night
And even watch me when I sleep;
I know You really love me dearly
And all Your promises to me You'll keep.

When I lie in bed and think of You
My heart always feels so glad;
To know You and all of Your goodness
Means I will never have a reason to be sad.

And just to know that there are Angels,
Who protect me everywhere I go,
Reminds me of Your love for me
And why I love You so....

I really have nothing to worry about.
I know I can always trust in You,
Because You are the one Who made me
And You will keep me safe, too!

Chapter Three
The Deceitfulness of Riches

The Mysterious Money

Kristen looked out the window of her bedroom hoping that the car she heard driving up into the driveway was her friend Sarah. She and Sarah had become best friends as soon as they had met in Sunday School class last year. Almost every Saturday they would visit one another and spend the day playing whatever they agreed suited the day best. Today was going to be no exception. Sarah had promised Kristen to be at her house no later than 10:00 a.m. and it was ten minutes to ten now.

Kristen could see that it wasn't Sarah's car in the driveway, but she wasn't the least bit disappointed when she saw Grandma getting out of the car. Grandma and Kristen had a special relationship. She loved to visit Grandma because she always had chores around the house that she would pay Kristen for doing. Last visit they made cookies for some of the neighbors and

Kristen delivered them herself. That made her feel especially good inside because she knew that it brought joy to the neighbors and it pleased God because they were caring for others.

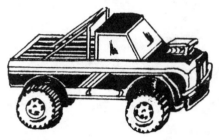

Kristen heard her little brother Josh downstairs; "Gam-ma, Gam-ma!!" he was saying excitedly.

"Josh is only two years old and he is always excited to see Grandma too!" thought Kristen. She ran downstairs to meet Grandma as fast as she could. She jumped over a toy truck on the bottom step and met Mom, Josh, and Grandma in the living room.

"Hello, Kristen, how's my favorite cookie baker today?" she asked with a smile.

"Just fine" answered Kristen. "Did you come to take me home with you?" Kristen inquired.

Grandma laughed, "Not today, honey. Besides Mom already told me Sarah will be over in just a few minutes. I know that you two have a big day planned. You are blessed to have such a good Christian friend to play with. I really just came by to give you something that I forgot to give you last week when you spent the night with me."

"Did I leave my toothpaste or something?" Kristen looked puzzled.

Grandma held out her hand and she wasn't holding toothpaste either! It was a crisp green twenty dollar bill. Kristen gasped "Grandma, is this really for me? I've never had this much money in my life!"

Grandma put her arm around Kristen and said, "I am 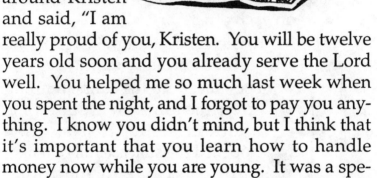 really proud of you, Kristen. You will be twelve years old soon and you already serve the Lord well. You helped me so much last week when you spent the night, and I forgot to pay you anything. I know you didn't mind, but I think that it's important that you learn how to handle money now while you are young. It was a special thing you did to spend your whole day baking cookies for other people, and then delivering them for me. I wanted to do something really special for you."

Just then there was a loud honking outside and a car drove up. Sarah got out of the car and came running down the walk toward the house.

"Well, I had better be going now, Kristen. I just want to say, remember to spend it wisely and don't forget to give God 10% of it first," Grandma said, as she gave Kristen and Josh a hug.

Josh spoke up, "Gam-ma take me home wif woo."

Mom answered for Grandma, "Not today Josh. Sarah is coming in the door and you can play with her and Kristen. Grandma has to go home now and we have to change your diaper."

Grandma left. Sarah came inside with a big smile on her face. "Hi Kristen. Sorry I'm late but I was packing all my mom's old makeup. She said I could bring it, and we could practice on each other!"

Kristen's face lit up, "Great!" she said. "Let's get started!"

They raced up the stairs jumping over the same toy truck on the bottom step. Just as they opened the suitcase full of make-up Josh came in the room. Sarah said, "Hey Josh, go get that truck on the stairs and you can play with it."

"Good idea" chimed Kristen. "Maybe he will get busy and forget about us."

Josh didn't forget. Soon he was back upstairs in Kristen's room, truck in hand. Not long after, he had lipstick smeared from head to toe. The girls tried to ignore him as much as possible.

"Hey I have a neat idea; let's go get some of my mom's old clothes that have big pockets like they used to wear in the old days. Then we can carry the makeup with us in our pockets, and Josh can't get to it," Kristen said as she headed downstairs.

Josh heard Kristen's idea and he repeated after her, "Pocket...pocket...pocket."

Sarah laughed at Josh. You don't have any pockets, Josh. Diapers don't have pockets!" Then she joined Kristen downstairs in her mother's bedroom closet.

"Here Kristen, this is a dress I used to wear when your father and I were dating. He would really be surprised to see you wearing it." She held up another one. It was bright blue and had big red buttons down the front and the largest pockets on the front that Sarah had ever seen. "This one is for you, Sarah; it might be a little big, but I think it will serve the purpose." They all laughed at how funny the clothes looked.

"Mom, I can't believe you really wore this stuff," Kristen giggled. Sarah began to laugh also and soon they were all in tears from laughing so hard.

"I guess it is pretty funny, but it didn't seem so at the time that I wore them. In fact your dad thought I was the prettiest girl in our class at school. Anyway you will probably be laughing at what you wear today in a few years. That is what my mom always told me and she was right. Speaking of Grandma, Kristen, what did you do with the money she gave you?" Mom asked with a look of concern.

Kristen thought for a moment. Then she ran upstairs as fast as she could. There was nothing upstairs but an empty suitcase and makeup scattered all over the floor. She came downstairs and back into her mother's bedroom in tears.

"It's gone, Mother, it's gone and I don't have any idea what I did with it. I had it when Sarah walked in the door and that was the last time I saw it..." Kristen cried.

Sarah explained, "Maybe it was some kind of...mysterious money monster that sneaked in the house when we weren't looking and gobbled it up!"

"Sarah!" Mother exclaimed, "I am surprised at you. You know good and well that there is no such thing as a monster. That's the silliest thing I've ever heard. It sounds like you've been watching too much television to me!" Sarah blushed and said, "I guess you're right!"

Kristen jumped up off the bed. "Josh!" she screamed. "He probably has it."

They all ran to Josh's room where he was sitting quietly on the floor playing with a set of building blocks. He smiled innocently and said, "Hi Kisten...play block?"

Mom looked at Josh in disgust, "Josh, you are covered with lipstick. It will take hours to get all of this off of you!"

Josh put his hands to his cheeks and giggled.

Kristen questioned Josh, "Do you have some money? or a green piece of paper?"

Josh ignored her completely. Just then the phone rang. Kristen ran to answer it. "Sarah! It was your mom and she is coming to get you. Your neighbor, Mrs. Kelley, wants you to babysit for a couple of hours," she explained.

"OK" replied Sarah. "Sorry I can't help you look anymore, but I really like babysitting for Mrs. Kelley. She is a real nice lady and I love playing with her baby."

"Let's go up stairs in my room and I will help you pick up all the makeup," Kristen said. "When I come to your house next week we can play with it again if it's all right with your mom."

It seemed like less than five minutes when Sarah's mom rang the doorbell and Sarah had to leave. Sarah and Kristen had cleaned up Kristen's room thoroughly and didn't find a trace of the twenty dollar bill anywhere. Now that Sarah was gone, Kristen would continue her search.

Kristen went into the kitchen where Mother was trying to get the lipstick off of Josh. He thought it was a funny game. Mother was not nearly as excited as Josh. She had a washcloth in one hand and a bar of soap in the other. She stopped scrubbing long enough to give Kristen some advice.

"Why don't you think back to when Grandma gave you the money. Then try to remember everything you did after that and trace your steps. Go everywhere that you were before. I believe that you will remember where you put it," she said.

"I think that is a great idea, Mom," Kristen replied.

Kristen went to the front door where Grandma had handed her the money. She remembered having the money in her hand when Sarah walked in with her suitcase full of make-up. She traced her steps back upstairs and looked around carefully to make sure that she didn't drop it on her way up. There was no clue so far...she thought, "When I decided to go ask Mom for some clothes, Sarah was up here alone with Josh. And if Josh doesn't have my money, then Sarah must have taken it!!! That's it. That is why she made up that ridiculous story about some mysterious money monster gobbling up my money. After all I did think it was rather strange that she had to leave so soon after she got here too."

Kristen got very, very angry. She ran downstairs and told Mom about her conclusion. "I will never speak to Sarah again," she said. "Can you believe that my best friend would do such a thing? Grandma will be so upset with me and it's all her fault. I don't even want to go to church tomorrow because I don't want to see her again."

Kristen's mother couldn't believe what she was hearing. How could Kristen turn on her very best friend and accuse her of such an awful thing. "Money should not be that important to anyone," she thought. She turned to Kristen and said, "Grandma was right, Kristen; you do need to learn how to handle money in the right way. You should never let money become so important to you that it ruins your friendship with others. You have no proof that Sarah took that money and you shouldn't falsely accuse her. I am going to put Josh in the tub and see if I can get the rest of this lipstick off of him. I hope by the time I come back you have asked God to forgive you for letting twenty dollars be more important to you than your best friend."

Mom left the room and Kristen began to cry. "I am really sorry, God," she prayed. "Please forgive me for being so hateful and accusing Sarah of doing wrong. If I never see that money again I will not blame anyone else for my mistakes. Please help me to be a better friend to Sarah...."

"Kristen! Kristen!" Mom called from the bathroom. "Come in here quick. I have something to show you."

Kristen ran to the bathroom and there in Mom's hand was the twenty dollar bill. "Guess what I found in Josh's diaper?" she laughed.

Josh looked at Kristen and said, "Josh have pocket too!"

Then Kristen understood what happened. Josh heard them talking about putting their makeup in a pocket so he couldn't get it. Josh thought that his diaper made a nice pocket!

Kristen was so glad that she had asked God to forgive her for her wrong attitude about money. But most of all she was glad that Sarah didn't know she had accused her of taking the money.

The next morning Kristen took her two dollars in tithe to church with her. She smiled a special smile at Sarah as she gave her offering. Somehow she felt closer to Sarah today than ever and she knew she would never again let money become more important than God or her friends.

The Deceitfulness of Riches Devotional
Exodus 20:1-3

God has blessed us with many wonderful things on this earth. They were put here for us to enjoy. There is nothing wrong with money or even being rich as long as God is always first place in your life and you let Him guide you in what to do with your money. It is important that we always give God tithe of all the money that we receive. You should never fall into the trap of loving money. Our love belongs to God. Money is just a tool to use for God.

Kristen's grandmother was very generous to give her granddaughter such a nice gift. Kristen made a terrible mistake when the money she received became more important than her friendship with Sarah. Kristen should have trusted in God to help her find the money she had misplaced instead of blaming its disappearance on others. Never let the enemy trick you into putting money before your family or friends. Remember the first commandment, to love God with all your heart.

Pray This Prayer Today....

Father,

Thank you for blessing me with all the good things that You have put here on the earth. I am glad that You want me to prosper and be healthy. Please help me to always remember not to love money, but to use it for Your glory. I will always be willing to give when You ask me to and because I do give, it will be given back unto me. (Luke 6:38) I want to use the money that You give me to help people and not to hurt them.

In Jesus' Name. Amen

If I Had A Million Dollars

If I had a million dollars
And didn't have Jesus in my heart,
The money wouldn't help me:
I just wouldn't know where to start.

I could never buy my way to heaven
Or buy happiness you see;
The only way to heaven
Is through Christ Who set me free.

I have found a much better way
Than loving the money God gives to me;
I give ten percent back to Him,
And He blesses me abundantly.

Then I have everything I need;
I never have to worry what I will eat.

God takes care of me daily,
And every one of my needs He will meet.

Money is a blessing used correctly.
It helps me in this life,
But I don't love my money.
Loving money only causes strife.

Chapter Four
The Desire of Other Things

Daniel's Doghouse

Daniel came rushing in the house, blue eyes sparkling.

"Mother! Mother! Can I please have just one more doggie biscuit for Teddy? He is so hungry; we have been playing all day. Besides, you know how much he loves doggie biscuits!"

"Oh, Daniel," sighed Mom. "You and that dog are something else! I guess Teddy can have one more treat; then you need  to come in the house and wash up for dinner. You can play with Teddy again tomorrow."

Daniel left as quickly as he had come. Only this time he had a huge smile on his face just thinking about how happy Teddy would be to get another treat. He loved the way Teddy's eyes danced and his tail wagged everytime he was excited.

Dad was coming in the door as Daniel was going out. "Hi Son," he said. "Off to play with Teddy again?" "Yes sir, but I'll be in for dinner in just a few minutes."

Dad walked quickly to the kitchen and gave Mom a big hug. "Is dinner ready?" he asked. "I'm really hungry."

"Yes, as soon as Daniel comes inside, we are ready to eat," she replied.

Daniel's Dad spoke up, "I have never seen a boy love a dog as much as he loves Teddy. I don't think anything could ever come between those two."

"I don't either!" agreed Mom. "It has been almost a year since you found Teddy on the side of the road. He and Daniel became best pals on the first day. I don't know how anyone could abandon such a cute and lovable little puppy. It seems like his curly hair, floppy ears and big brown eyes would make anyone love him."

Daniel came in and they sat down to dinner. Mom asked Daniel, "Did you know it has been almost a year since Dad found Teddy? It seems like yesterday."

"Yes Ma'am. It will be a year next week. I've been thinking about a present for him for a while. I have the perfect thing in mind."

"What's that Daniel?" Mom asked with a smile.

"A big doghouse, with a sign on it that says, 'TEDDY' right above the door. He will love it and I am going to make it myself. I have been saving my money for weeks to buy the lumber. Don't you think it is a great idea?"

"Well, I don't guess anyone can argue with that," laughed Dad. "In fact," he said, "I will take you to the lumber yard after dinner and you can buy all the things you need. It will be a wonderful experience for you to build something by yourself!"

To Daniel it seemed like hours before dinner was over and the dishes were washed. Everytime the large hand on the clock moved another notch Daniel became more and more excited. He thought, "This will be the BEST present I have ever given to Teddy!"

Dad interrupted his thoughts, "It's time to go...."

It was the beginning of an exciting adventure. Hours went by before Dad and Daniel returned home. Finally, Mom saw the flash of lights shine through the window as she heard the roar of the engine die down. She ran out to meet them and asked, "Well, how did it go, Daniel?"

Daniel uncovered the lumber in the back of the pickup truck.

"OH MY," she gasped. "Are you sure you're not building an extra room onto the house?"

Daniel laughed. "No Mom, it's just that...well...I just want Teddy to have the best doghouse in town. I want him to know how much he is loved."

Dad spoke up, "It's time to go to bed now, Son. I will unload this lumber later. It's time for you to get some sleep."

Daniel lay in bed thinking of how he would build the doghouse. He could see himself nailing the boards together one by one. He could hear Teddy outside...ruff-ruff...ruff...he never barked too loudly, just enough to let Daniel know that he would rather be in the house with him. Daniel couldn't help but smile thinking of how proud Teddy would be of his new doghouse.

The morning sunlight glistened through the window panes as Daniel rubbed his sleepy eyes. "OH! I have so much to do...I must get started." He jumped out of bed, dressed himself and raced downstairs in record time.

Dad was at the breakfast table drawing something on a large sheet of paper. "Here, Son," he said with a smile. "I stayed up late last night drawing plans for the doghouse. These pictures and instructions should help you with your first construction job."

"Thanks Dad," Daniel said as he gave him a quick hug. Then he grabbed the hammer and a big brown sack of nails and ran outside to begin his new project.

Teddy ran to meet Daniel as he opened the back door. He had a small orange ball in his mouth and was trying his best to get Daniel to notice.

"No Teddy," Daniel spoke sharply. "I can't play now. I have to work on a surprise."

Teddy watched enthusiastically for a while hoping that soon Daniel would be finished. He waited, but Daniel just kept right on hammering on the silly looking box. Finally Teddy decided to find something else to do.

It was late evening and Daniel had worked all day long. He had barely taken time to eat lunch. Mom looked over the white picket fence and said, "Daniel, it is time to come in. Dad's home from work and dinner is on the table. We can't wait any longer. You can work on the doghouse tomorrow."

"Yes Ma'am," said Daniel.

Mom could tell from the tone of his voice that he was not happy about having to quit.

At the dinner table Dad asked Daniel how the house was coming along.

"It is going great. I can understand your diagrams really well, and I think I can have it finished by next week. Can you go outside with me later and look at what I've finished so far?" Daniel asked.

"Sure," replied Dad proudly. "I'm anxious to see how my son the carpenter is doing."

Daniel was eating as fast as he could. Mom looked at him. "Son," she said, "just slow down. The doghouse will be there when you finish eating." They all laughed!!

When dinner was finally over Dad and Daniel carried their plates to the kitchen sink. Mom smiled and said, "You two go on outside, I'll clean up the dishes tonight. I know you have a lot to talk about."

Daniel headed toward the back door. "Thanks, Mom, that was the best meal ever. You're really a good cook. Bye." The door closed quickly.

Teddy again met Daniel at the door as soon as he stepped out. This time he had a stick in his mouth. Sometimes Daniel would throw the stick as far as he could and Teddy would retrieve it. That was the game Teddy had in mind as he looked at Daniel wagging his tail in excitement. But Daniel ignored Teddy once again. All he seemed to care about was hammering on the box. Teddy gave up on Daniel and found himself an old bone to chew on. "Tomorrow he will play with me," Teddy thought.

Tomorrow came and Teddy waited for Daniel to bring his food. Every morning he always scratched his head as he gave him his dogfood. Teddy could hardly wait. After he ate all of his food he knew Daniel would have some doggie biscuits, too!!!

Daniel was so busy thinking about the doghouse he almost forgot to feed Teddy. But, he remembered when he saw the empty dish. "Sorry, Teddy," he said, "I don't have time to play today. I've got more work to do." He scratched Teddy once behind the ears and didn't even remember the doggie biscuits.

Six days went by. Everyday it was the same. Daniel was just too busy to play games anymore. Teddy felt like no one needed him. Teddy didn't meet him at the door that morning.

Nighttime came and Daniel went to bed knowing that tomorrow was the big day. Mom and Dad were excited too! "Teddy will have been with us for one year tomorrow...he is going to love his present," thought Daniel as he drifted off to sleep. Funny thing though...he didn't hear Teddy barking as usual. "Oh well, he must be tired too." Daniel closed his eyes and dreamed of Teddy's new doghouse.

Morning finally came and Mom shook Daniel gently. "Daniel," she said, "Today is the big day. Dad painted the rest of the doghouse last night and it's ready. It is in the garage. Get up and you can see how it looks."

Daniel jumped out of bed and ran to the garage. He could just see Teddy's tail wagging and the excitement he would feel as he saw his new doghouse. It was beautiful. Dad had painted it white with a red roof. There was a sign hung over the door that said "TEDDY" in big red letters. "No dog could ask for more," thought Daniel to himself.

He ran to open the door and let Teddy in the garage to see his anniversary present. But Teddy wasn't at the door as usual. Daniel called but Teddy didn't come. He walked to the fence and there was a great big hole under the fence. "DAD!" cried Daniel, "come quick, Teddy's gone!!!"

Mom and Dad ran outside. Dad shook his head. "Son, I'm afraid you gave too much time to building the  doghouse and forgot about loving Teddy. I knew he was sad but I never dreamed he would run away. You were giving him a better gift than a doghouse. You were giving him yourself and he missed that this week when you were too busy for him."

Mom hugged Daniel as he cried. "Don't worry, honey; we will find him" she said hopefully.

Mom walked toward town to look for Teddy. Daniel stayed in the yard in case he came back and Dad went to all the neighbors' houses asking if anyone had seen him.

Daniel had a lot of time to think while Mom and Dad were gone. He prayed that God would help them find Teddy. He thought to himself, "If Teddy ever comes back I will always remember to play with him. I will never again get too busy to love him."

"Daniel, Daniel!" it was Mom calling. "I found him, I found Teddy." She was holding him in her arms as she ran to the backyard. Teddy licked Daniel in the face and Daniel was so happy to see him he didn't even mind.

"I love you, Teddy. I love you..." Daniel said as he picked up the orange ball and threw it. Teddy jumped and ran as fast as he could across the grass after the ball. He was so happy and so was Daniel.

Daniel never did get Teddy to sleep in the doghouse that he had worked on so diligently. But he kept it in the backyard as a reminder that things are not as important as they may seem, but love is always important.

The Desire of Other Things Devotional
Matthew 6:33

Daniel loved Teddy with all of his heart. He wanted to make him happy more than anything. He thought a doghouse would make Teddy happy. Teddy didn't want a new doghouse. All he wanted was for Daniel to love him. Sometimes, people try to make God happy by working hard and doing good deeds. Nothing is wrong with good deeds, but God wants our love. Things shouldn't get in the way of our love for God. We should always put God first and remember to talk to Him everyday. Reading the Bible is important also. This helps us to know God better.

Pray This Prayer Today....

Father,

Thank You for loving me so much. I want to please You more than anything. Please help me to always put You first in everything I do. I want to serve You with my whole heart and not let other things come between us. Thank You for sending Your Holy Spirit to remind me of Your love for me and for helping me to remember to always put You first.

In Jesus' Name. Amen

I Choose To Love God First

When I look around me
And see all the beautiful things You've made,
I know why the birds sing songs
And I know why Daniel always prayed.

When I look up to the sky
And see the stars You placed up there,
I can understand how David slew Goliath
Instead of running away really scared.

I know that Noah must have known You
The same way that I do
Because he believed You and built that ark
And I choose to believe you too.

Shadrack, Meshack, and Abedniego never
were afraid,
The were very brave indeed,
They chose to obey You,
And You delivered them in their time of need.

All these people chose to put You first;
They refused to love anything more than You.
I want to be like them God;
I choose to love You first too!

Seed Sown On Good Soil

And these are they which are sown
on good ground;
such as hear the word, and receive it,
and bring for the fruit,
some thirtyfold, some sixty,
and some an hundred.

Mark 4:20

Chapter Five
Seed Sown on Good Soil

The Pie That Caught Hubert's Eye

Jeffery loved going to Grandma's house! Grandma always cooked wonderful things to eat, and it seemed as if each trip was a little more exciting! "The farm is a great place to live," thought Jeffery. "I wonder what we will do there this weekend? Maybe Grandpa will take me fishing. I hope Grandma bakes my favorite apple pie!"

Just then Jeffery heard his mother call him. "Come on, Jeffery, it is time to go to Grandma's house. I'm supposed to drop you off in an hour. We really must hurry." And off they went.

As they arrived, Jeffery could see Grandma and Grandpa waving from the front porch. He

felt so lucky to have grandparents that loved him so much. He knew when he stepped out of the car they would have a big hug for him. And as always, they did!!

Jeffery waved goodbye to his mother and ran into the house to see what Grandma had baking. He could hardly believe his eyes! There was one, two, three apple pies. "Wow," yelled Jeffery so loudly that Grandma came running.

"Oh, Jeffery!" she exclaimed, "you scared me!"

"Do I get to eat all of these?" he replied.

"No, I'm afraid not, Jeffery. But one of them is for after supper tonight. The other two are for the children's orphanage in town. We are going to drive in and take these pies to the children this afternoon. You see, some children don't have a family like you do. And sometimes it is nice for them to have a pretend Grandma like me bring them something special to eat. Would you like to go with me?"

"Sure!" said Jeffery.

Grandma took the pies out of the oven and put them in the window to cool. The wonderful smell of baked apples and cinnamon filled the house. Then suddenly, Jeffery heard Grandma screaming like he had never heard her scream before!

"You come back here!" she yelled. "You'll never get away with this!"

Jeffery couldn't imagine what could have happened. Grandma called to Jeffery, "Hurry and get Grandpa — someone just stole one of my apple pies."

Grandpa and Jeffery were too late. Grandma was the only one who saw the thief. "Oh, if I ever get my hands on that boy I'll...I'll...well, I don't know what I will do! But there is one thing I do know...there won't be any pie for us for supper tonight! There are ten children at the orphanage and it will take two pies to feed all of them. I surely will not have time to bake another one. We will just have to do without."

On the way to the orphanage Jeffery thought of how good those pies would taste. He knew Grandma was right to give them to the orphanage. After all, they don't have a grand-mother like he does.

When they arrived, the director of the orphanage introduced each boy and girl to Jeffery and Grandma. Sally, Karen, John, Bill, Casey, Lynn, Bobby, Robert, Jason, and...Hubert. Boy, Hubert sure acts scared thought Jeffery. He looks as white as a sheet. I wonder what could be wrong?

Grandma whispered to Jeffery, "Hubert is the boy who stole my pie today. Shhh...keep it quiet."

"But...but...Grandma what shall we do?"

After everyone had finished his pie, Grandma took Hubert and Jeffery by the hand and the three of them went into an empty room. Would Grandma SPANK him? Would she call the police? NO!

When they closed the door she gave Hubert a great big hug. As tears came to her eyes she said, "Hubert, I forgive you for stealing my pie."

Hubert said, "You mean you won't tell?"

"No," she said, "I won't tell, because if someone really forgives you, they also forget that it happened."

Hubert couldn't believe his ears. She knew he stole the pie and she wasn't going to tell! "Why, no one has ever done anything like that for me." Hubert was amazed.

"Yes, Hubert, someone did...many years ago. A man named Jesus died on a cross for your sin, so God could forgive every bad thing you have ever done. Jesus was the Son of God

and the Bible says if you will believe on Him and confess Him as your Lord you will be saved. Then God will change your heart and you will want to do right instead of wrong."

Jeffery spoke softly, "Grandma, I would like to ask Jesus into my heart! Can we do it now?"

Hubert exclaimed, "Me too!"

Grandma took both boys' hands and prayed. Right there Jesus came into their hearts.

From then on everytime Jeffery visited Grandma he had a very special friend to call. Hubert and Jeffery would always remember how the pie that caught Hubert's eye changed their lives!

Seed Sown On Good Soil
Devotional
Romans 2:4

Hubert heard of Christ's forgiveness by Grandma forgiving him so easily. The Bible says it is the goodness of God that leads men to repentance. When Hubert and Jeffery realized how much Christ loved them, they both gave their hearts to Him. Grandma sowed the Word in their hearts and BOTH of them believed on Christ and received Him into their hearts. I am sure that Hubert and Jeffery won many of their friends to Christ as well. You can see that telling one person about Jesus can win a lot of people to Christ. God will multiply His Word when it is sown in people's hearts. Remember how good God really is, and let His goodness shine through you!

Pray This Prayer Today....

Father,

Thank You for giving us Your Word (The Bible) to read. I thank You that as I read it, I grow closer to You. Please help my heart to be good ground. When I hear Your Word, I want to be a doer of it and not just a hearer only. Thank You for helping me to produce good things in my life and to let Your light shine through me.

In Jesus' Name. Amen

I Want To Be Good Ground

I am so thankful to You God,
For all the good things You have done.
You loved me so much,
Though I was a sinner, You gave Your
Only Son.

Now I've given You my heart,
I want to live every day for You
As I listen to Your Word,
I will be a hearer and a doer of it, too.

This is the way I will be; like seed,
Sown on good ground.
I will produce a very good crop
And be a blessing to all those around.

Other Books by Beverly Capps Burgess

Faith Tales
Chicken Little Conquers Fear
The Three Bears In Ministry
The Three Little Pigs
Little Red Ridinghood
Little Red Hen
Jack & The Beanstalk

Books That Teach Relationship With God
God, Are You Really Real?
Is Easter Just For Bunnies?
God Is My Best Friend
How Can I Please You, God?
God Is Never Too Busy To Listen

Pre-School Curriculum
Friends with God — Volume 1
God's Word Is Truth — Volume 2
Obedience And Forgiveness — Volume 3

For More Information
Call Or Write To:
Beverly Burgess Ministries
P.O. Box 520
Broken Arrow, OK 74013
1-800-388-5437